MW00988334

# GOD MATH

# GOD MATH

*What to Do When the Numbers Don't Add Up*

MILTON CAMPBELL

© 2017 Milton Campbell
All rights reserved.

ISBN: 1548464678
ISBN 13: 9781548464677

# DEDICATION

*This book is truly a gracious reminder to me that God is able. The reality that God would allow and resource me to be able to put a small part of my unworthy story in print is astounding. The thought that one person may be brought closer to Jesus is a miracle in itself. I am humbled that the Lord has blessed me with so much more than I deserve. I have an amazing biological and spiritual family. I am privilege to pastor the most amazing congregation on the planet. My first flock are my wife Christina and daughters Malia and Moriah. The Lord teaches me so much through my interactions with each of you daily. Second only to Jesus, you are my greatest treasure. To The Midtown Bridge Church family, I am forever grateful for your love and patience extended toward me as I learn how to pastor. Only the Lord could have chosen such a gracious people for me to share life with.*

*To my mother, who is with Jesus in Heaven, your legacy of faithfulness to the Lord established my bedrock in the Lord. Wish you were here to share this chapter of my life, but I know you are where we all long to be. To my brothers Aaron and Eric, sister Angelle, parents Daddy Keith & Mama Nina, and friend Anthony, you have been a constant support and source of encouragement well before I knew anything about influence or platforms. You have had my back at so many turns.*

*To my aunts, uncles, cousins, coaches, pastors and friends, I am forever grateful that the Lord has invested so much into this unworthy earthen vessel. You are a constant reminder of God's grace being extended toward me. I pray that God cause all grace to abound to you, so that you always have all sufficiency in everything, you may have an abundance for every good deed. (2 Cor.9:8)*

# CONTENTS

Introduction· · · · · · · · · · · · · · · · · · · · · · · · · · · · · · · · · · · ix

God Math and Time · · · · · · · · · · · · · · · · · · · · · · · · · · · · 1
God Math and Relationships· · · · · · · · · · · · · · · · · · · · 31
God Math and Money· · · · · · · · · · · · · · · · · · · · · · · · · · 45
God Math at Its Greatest · · · · · · · · · · · · · · · · · · · · · · · 59

Conclusion· · · · · · · · · · · · · · · · · · · · · · · · · · · · · · · · · · · 69
30 Days of Reflection · · · · · · · · · · · · · · · · · · · · · · · · · · 71
About Milton · · · · · · · · · · · · · · · · · · · · · · · · · · · · · · · · · 103

# INTRODUCTION

We learn mathematical absolutes at an early age. As early as preschool, we are trained to learn math facts like these:

$$1 + 1 = 2 \qquad 2 + 2 = 4 \qquad 5 + 5 = 10$$
$$10 + 10 = 20 \qquad 20 + 20 = 40$$

These are considered absolutes, mathematically speaking. Because we know this is true, we are naturally wired to think that math always works this way. We move through our formative years believing that this is always true. Then God steps in and troubles the water of our mathematical absolutes. You see, God's mathematical system is quite different from ours.

In God's mathematical system, two fish feed over five thousand (John 6). In God's mathematical system, one small quart of oil fills up several hundred gallons (2 Kings 4). In God's mathematical system, 300 warriors defeat 135,000 foot soldiers (Judg. 8). Simply put, God's mathematical system defies logic.

What is God math? God math is when ordinary people obey God in ordinary ways and experience extraordinary outcomes. God math is the undeniable intervention of God in ordinary situations. We cannot force God math to happen or predict whether it will happen, but it is undeniable when it does happen. As you read the following pages, my greatest hope for you is that you will start to be faithful in the everyday experiences of life. This is an invitation into the ordinary but with anticipation that you will experience the extraordinary.

This book is about more than living a life of great faith, though that is a focus; it is about practical obedience. Many people may never see God do the extraordinary because they struggle with obedience in the ordinary. I invite you to take a walk as we examine the lives of some ordinary men and women whom God allowed to experience extraordinary outcomes. Believe it or not, they were not that special from a cultural perspective. Few people in the Bible were exceptional. As a matter of fact, many of them were closer to the bottom of the societal echelon of their day—not all but certainly more than a few. What we will discover as we examine their lives is that ordinary obedience is often what God uses to accomplish extraordinary outcomes.

Join me on this journey as we learn together what God does through our everyday obedience in following Him. What I am discovering is how little control I have over the outcome, but my greatest responsibility is whether I have been faithful. God will not hold us accountable for being fruitful (making things grow), but we will be held accountable for being faithful (consistent and doing our best with what we have).

In the pages to follow, I hope to lay the groundwork for what I believe is one of the most exciting privileges of being a follower of Jesus Christ. Now, you may not be there yet, and that is okay (for now). Perhaps in reading this book, you may start to hear God calling you to Himself. At the very least, you will get a better understanding of some of the ideas that Christians believe about their God. I invite you to take this journey as we explore this idea of God math.

# GOD MATH
# AND TIME

The alarm goes off, and you are left to make that ever-so-dreadful decision. You know where this is going…do you hit snooze on the alarm and catch a few more minutes, or do you get up early to spend time with God? That is the struggle of any honest follower of Christ. In those moments, our minds tell us how much better we would feel with an extra ten, thirty, or sixty minutes of sleep. After all, we had a long day, and we deserve—*no*, we need our rest! Have you ever experienced the sleep tug-of-war? I know I have, and sleep has been the victor too many times. It seems that in those moments, the sandman has me in a headlock and will not let me go. (My WWA wrestling fans know what I mean.)

Our culture tells us how important sleep is to our health. Now, I am going to tread lightly because I am far from a man of science or medicine. I certainly see value in rest and believe it is biblical. However, too often rest stands in opposition to obedience. This is a delicate dance and certainly a tension to be managed. However, for the workaholics, I will come back to you later. In this section, I would like to address those who love sleep. I want to address one faulty idea: your body needs eight hours of sleep per night. Now, I agree theoretically that we should identify what our body needs, but we also must acknowledge this varies from person to person. We also must be careful not to put God in a box.

Let me give you an example. What if we were presented with the opportunity to be awarded $100,000 if we were to forgo sleep for three days or even seven days? Few people would walk away from that challenge. Why? No matter how much you and I love sleep, the reward of $100,000 outweighs the temporary satisfaction that sleep brings. In our minds, we would rationalize (and be correct) that we can recapture that sleep on an island once we have received our reward. As difficult as this challenge might be, we would push ourselves to attain the prize.

**Do not allow momentary pleasure to cause you to miss your truest treasure, which is intimacy with the God of heaven and earth.**

As much satisfaction that $100,000 can bring, it pales in comparison to the joy God brings. I know what you are likely thinking: "But I can tangibly feel the joy I receive from the $100,000. I could do practical good with the money and so much more." You are partially correct, but you are missing the most important truth we are invited into. Temporary delight pales in comparison to long-term joy. Do not allow momentary pleasure to cause you to miss your truest treasure, which is intimacy with the God of heaven and earth.

One of our most precious commodities is time. We can recover money and material possessions, but once time is spent, it never returns. You cannot get yesterday back. You can only redeem the moments at hand. What we do with our time says a lot about what we truly believe. How we leverage time says a lot about what we value. So what does this have to do with sleeping in? I am glad you asked.

Did you know that there are 8,760 hours in a calendar year? If you slept 8 hours a day, you would sleep 2,920 hours, which would leave 5,840 waking hours. If you worked 8 hours per day, 6 days a week, with no vacation, that would come to 2,496 hours, still leaving 3,344 waking hours. If you spent 4 hours a day, 6 days per week commuting, that would come to 1,248 hours, still leaving 2,096 waking hours remaining. If you spent 5 hours per day, 7 days per week with family or friends, it would come to 1,820 hours, still leaving 276 hours remaining. By now, you either feel excited or overwhelmed by these possibilities. Hopefully, you heard these statistics and came to the realization that you have more free time available than you thought! Perhaps you realized how much time you have available that could be reallocated toward accomplishing something greater.

What do we do with this new awareness? I hope that you are now starting to see that time with God is possible. Now, the danger is that we treat this as another checkbox on our to-do lists. However, that is not the aim or heart of what I am trying to persuade you to do. Rather, I believe that time with God will become the most critical part of your day. As we learn to give God a portion of our time, we truly learn how to be redemptive with our time. What do I mean by redemptive? I simply mean we use time the way it is supposed to be used. Let me provide an example.

I have two daughters. They are presently eight and ten years old as I write this book. My daughters love to play. They are quite content crowding their days with dolls, gymnastics, riding bikes, and playing school (periodically pausing to ask what is for lunch or dinner). They both are really good students, but the moment we tell them to pause and do actual schoolwork (though they were just playing school with their dolls), they pitch a fit! Why is that? It is because they are more hardwired to play than they are to push. They enjoy the celebration and encouragement they receive from good grades but do not necessarily love the sacrifice required to attain them. As parents, we have to train them how to push through moments of temporary delight so they can experience long-term joy.

Now back to the sleep tug-of-war. The alarm goes off, and everything in you says to hit the snooze button. Yet there is a still, small voice that says, "Arise, and meet with Me." Our temporary delight is strong in that moment; it tells us that we deserve or even that we need to rest. Yet we must push through temporary delight to experience long-term joy. What we stand to gain will be so much more rewarding than what we stand to lose. We must learn to *push*!

What God wants to invite you into is so much greater than the invitations we can write for ourselves. God's invitation is not limited to an outcome, but it is always greater knowledge of a Person. That Person is Him. The desired outcome is simply what He uses to get our attention (maybe to know that Person). Knowing Him changes how we view time. Knowing Him makes a world of difference in how we leverage our time. Imagine, if you will, being invited to spend the day with your hero. This is one who has prestige, power, and unimaginable resources at his or her disposal. How carefully would you hold on to every word this person shared with you? How much would you cherish every second with him or her? How confident would you be in your hero's insight and wisdom? Would you blow off the meeting with your hero because you need your eight hours of sleep? As a matter of fact, I imagine that you would get very little sleep the night before because of the excitement surrounding the opportunity.

If you have trusted in Christ as Lord and Savior, that is what we are invited into every morning. Don't let sleep deny you of the opportunity to experience Christ more fully. You may be concerned because this is not presently what you experience in your times with God. Again, I say, *push*. God sometimes allows seasons of distance to bring us into seasons of closeness. Seasons of distance are difficult but so rewarding if we see them from God's perspective.

*God sometimes allows seasons of distance*
*to bring us into seasons of closeness.*

My daughters started walking at ten and eleven months old. I remember the kind ladies in our nursery sharing with my wife: "This is the smallest I have ever seen a child walking." (Proud daddy moment, as you can tell.) However, those reading who are parents or have been around a child learning to walk can remember the process. First, you start by holding your child's hands and helping her to take her initial steps. Then, as she gets more comfortable, you move back and encourage her to walk toward you. It is one of the most exciting moments in a parent-child relationship. You watch with eager anticipation and expectation as that child gains confidence to move toward you with those wobbly legs. Each step, you cheer her on while possibly moving back to build her confidence. Remember how proud you were when that child made her first journey across the room and fell in your arms? I believe that is how God trains His children. When we feel that He is distant, He is teaching us how to walk by faith. When we feel God is distant, we are learning that He is our strength. **Seasons of distance are actually meant to bring us into seasons of closeness.**

The worse thing that could happen is that you and I give up in the midst of the process and forfeit true intimacy with God. A powerful picture is seen in Mark 14:32–42, where Jesus is with His disciples in the Garden of Gethsemane. The cross is imminent, yet Jesus takes His disciples aside to pray. This was another potent example of Jesus modeling intimacy with the Father. He invited His disciples to join Him in this prayer meeting, even if at a distance. However, in the sleep tug-of-war, the disciples lost the battle and fell asleep. We are provided another clear picture of how ordinary these men were whom Jesus chose. They were so much like you and me. Jesus comes to them three times and finds them sleeping. Hours later they would witness Jesus suspended between heaven and earth in the most heinous crime ever committed. They missed this moment to enjoy intimacy with Jesus because of sleep. Now, that is only an implication of that passage, but it is so worth noting. Might that be true of me? Might that be true of you? Only heaven truly knows how and if remaining awake would have changed their responses during the circumstances that would follow the Garden of Gethsemane's missed opportunity. One truth we cannot ignore is that God invites us into deeper intimacy with Him through our investment of time. That time we are asked to invest may often require sacrifice of sleep. Just as in marriage, intimacy is spelled *t-i-m-e*, so it is with God.

Many of you reading this book do not have a problem with sleeping too much. As a matter of fact, you perhaps land on the other end of the spectrum. Sleep is not on your radar. You are a worker bee and love getting things done. Efficiency is your primary love language. If that is you, then the next chapter will be of great value to you. However, before you move forward, take some time to ask God to show you what obedience looks like in this area. How might the God of heaven and earth be inviting you into a deeper and more vibrant relationship with Him? Could the small sacrifice of time be what He demands of you in this season?

# Swift

Let me now share some of the benefits of investing time with God. It is through our time with God that we truly come to learn how to manage the remainder of our time for daily activities. If you have been around church long enough, then you have likely heard some teaching on tithing. I will not spend too much time here (there is another chapter on money), but let me simply define "tithe." Its most basic definition is "a tenth part." The focus is to give the first 10 percent of our earnings to God. That leaves you with 90 percent. That is all I will say for now, because I imagine some may be getting uncomfortable. (It is okay—breathe!) I share that basic teaching because in a roundabout way, I believe the foundational teaching on tithing works with time. Now, there are no passages in the Bible that say we are to give God 10 percent of our time. That is not the part of the tithing principle to be gleaned. The purpose of the tithe is always about us and not about God needing anything from us. The primary purpose of the tithe is to remind us that God provides and that He is worth putting our trust in.

Now, let's take that idea and apply it to leveraging time. God provides, and He is worth putting our trust in. If God provides time, then certainly He is worth trusting in to show us how to manage it. This transforms how we manage our time, and it places urgency on who we spend time with. There are a couple of biblical characters who show how God math affected their leveraging of time.

There is this guy name Nehemiah recorded in the Bible. Nehemiah was an ordinary guy who lived around mid-400 BC. He was serving as cupbearer to King Artaxerxes, ruler of Persia. This was both a prestigious and dangerous position. It was prestigious because he had constant access to the king. However, it was dangerous because what better way to take the king out than by poisoning? Nehemiah would be considered quite successful during his day. He had seemingly climbed the corporate ladder. He was perhaps living the Persian dream. Then one day he is visited by relatives from his hometown of Jerusalem and asks a seemingly simple question about how the family is doing. Nehemiah learns that the family is struggling back home, and the city he loves is a disgrace. So Nehemiah rallies together an army, marches into Jerusalem, and kicks butt. That is probably how Hollywood would rewrite the story. However, that is not at all how the story unfolds. Nehemiah becomes overwhelmed with grief and concern for what is happening for many people who, up until this point, he had likely never met. Nehemiah does the most important thing one could do with one's time. He spends the next several months praying like crazy.

This is the first practical example of God math at work. **It is the undercurrent of prayer that leads to the tidal wave of change.**

*It is the undercurrent of prayer that leads
to the tidal wave of change.*

I am not a man of the water; as a matter of fact, I certainly prefer land. However, ocean swimmers are not most concerned about waves. Rather, more dangerous than waves are the undercurrents. Undercurrents are currents of water that flow under the surface of a large body of water. What makes them dangerous is that they can sweep swimmers underwater, causing them to drown as the current carries them along its path. A strong undercurrent carries the greatest of swimmers wherever it desires. Undercurrents can cause the most experienced of swimmers to drown.

Yet prayer is the undercurrent of power for those who follow God. Instead of harm, prayer helps us to do more than we thought possible because the God of the sea and land is working on our behalf. Prayer causes us to be swept into the activity of God carrying us into His providential will. Undercurrents move you faster than you can go on your own. Prayer does the same thing. We have this faulty idea that prayer slows us down, when in actuality it speeds us up. Unfortunately, too often we give up on prayer because we see it as a time waster when it is actually a time-saver. As calculated as our plans may be, even the greatest of strategists lacks the wisdom of the sovereign God.

I have an extensive background competing in athletics. My sport of choice is track and field. I started running when I was eight years old and competed on all levels, ranging from youth up to the professional arena. I was graced to win several NCAA

Championships, USA National Championships, and several World Championships and take part in setting a World Record. I experienced much success and failure during my career. There was one training tool we used frequently in my development through the years. It was known as the speed harness. This little tool was very effective in preparing me to reach peak performance. I know you are pondering how it worked. It worked by strapping one end of the harness around your waist, and the other end would be held by a coach. There were two options for use. Typically, we would start with the harness behind us and the coach in tow, providing painful resistance.

It always started off fun, but around the fourth or fifth repetition, things became extremely difficult! The resistance the coach provided caused my muscles to burn and fatigue to set in, resulting in tremendous pain. Though the finish line was physically a few meters away, the resistance caused it to feel as if it were a mile off.

That is what prayer feels like at times. We cry out to the Lord to increase our finances, to heal a loved one, or to mend a broken relationship. Yet it seems as if nothing is happening. The desired outcome seems to be moving further away from us. We start to lose heart or think that God cares little about our situation. The pain of pushing through seems too difficult for us to keep going.

Remember that I mentioned there was a second option for the speed harness use. That same harness could easily be rotated around to where the coach was in front of me. Now instead of the coach providing resistance, he would now provide assistance. That is when it became fun again. In the resistance phase, I felt restricted and held back. However, in the assistance phase, I felt unimaginable freedom. I would begin to run at a pace that I could not do without assistance from the harness.

*Prayer positions us for divine enablement, allowing us to accomplish far more than we ever thought possible.*

So it is with prayer that we learn to push through. We start to see God work through us to accomplish things we *know* could not happen without Him. Prayer positions us for divine enablement, allowing us to accomplish far more than we ever thought possible. Such was the case with Nehemiah. I left off sharing how he became burdened by the condition of his family back in Jerusalem. He entered into a season of prayer and diligently seeking direction from God in chapter 1 of Nehemiah. God first grants him favor by moving on the king's heart to fund the building project in chapter 2. I will revisit that later. In the midst of tremendous opposition (chapters 4–5), Nehemiah leads the people to rebuild the walls of Jerusalem in fifty-two days (chapter 6). The magnitude of this building project overwhelmingly points to divine assistance. In chapter 1 he gets a burden, and by chapter 6, he has completed the building project in record time. What was happening? God math! Nehemiah 6:16 tells us all we need to know. It says, "When all our enemies heard of it, and all the nations surrounding us saw it, they lost their confidence; for they recognized that this work had been accomplished with the help of our God" (NASB).

Not only did those taking part in the work recognize the hand of God but even those who opposed the work recognized the hand of God. God math works that way. **We can't force it to happen or predict when it will, but it is undeniable when it does.**

I am learning how to put God first when it comes to my time. I have seen this happen so often in my life. Even as I write this book, it is an example of God math. When I finally gave this project back to God, within the first seventy-two hours, I was able to write 30 percent of this book. (Hopefully you are not saying, "Well, you should have taken more time!") Have you ever had a moment where the day ahead of you looked impossible? You dreaded getting up to face the day because there was so much awaiting completion. Perhaps it was so overwhelming that you had no idea where to even start. In that moment, you thought God would have to take a back seat, and you would get time in with Him maybe later. However, that small voice whispered, "You know later will not come." After further nudging from that voice, you decided to try to squeeze ten minutes of Bible reading and prayer in. However, something happened that you did not anticipate during that time with God. God math! You arose with greater clarity and focus. You knew you were still facing a colossal to-do list, but for some reason, you felt equipped. That is the God math effect.

***Even before the outcome, we have a new outlook.*** I am certainly not the most efficient guy. However, I have noticed that when I give God control of my time, things that usually take me two or three days to complete take two or three hours. Perhaps you charge it to luck, but if you knew me, then you would know that it requires more than luck, given my propensity for distractions. If you don't believe me, I suggest you put God to the test.

This is a truth that has taken me years to realize. There is nothing that I am better at than God. Contemplate on that for a moment. *Nothing!* Since God is better with managing my time than I am, it behooves me to let Him guide me in how I manage it. I invite you to take the God math time challenge.

# *GOD MATH TIME CHALLENGE*

1.  Commit to carving out at least fifteen minutes per day to spend with God. Make it the first thing you do when you awake.

2.  Practice praying over your schedule at the start of your day.

3.  Keep a journal or note pad to record how God works over the next thirty days. (Feel free to write in the margins of this book.)

# Slow

I must present my case in balance because life does not always turn out like Nehemiah's experience. God math worked favorably to speed Nehemiah up. However, there are times when God math works to slow us down. There are times when God takes His time (pun intended). There are moments where God's eternal clock seems to be broken, or at least we feel that way. How should we respond in moments like these? Three truths will help us to faithfully persevere during these types of seasons.

First, understand that you are not the first and highly unlikely the last person to feel this way. As a matter of fact, there were several people in the Bible who felt this way. Peter was one of the men in Jesus' inner circle while Jesus walked the earth. Peter wrote a couple of books in the Bible. In one of those books, 2 Peter 3:8–9, he writes, "But do not let this one fact escape your notice, beloved, that with the Lord one day is like a thousand years and a thousand years like one day. The Lord is not slow about His promise, as some count slowness, but is patient toward you, not wishing for any to perish but for all to come to repentance." Peter writes to encourage followers of Jesus who were experiencing tremendous suffering for their faith. They had been faithful, and it seemed that the more faithful they were, the more they suffered. Time was not working in their favor. Peter writes to remind them of how God views time. I believe the heart of Peter's encouragement to them and us is this: **when God moves slow, it is a prime opportunity for us to grow!**

Sometimes God gives swift growth, while most of the time, He gives slow growth. Peter provides good news in the midst of the bad. Peter assures them that God will reward their obedience and repay their opposition. To be honest, that is hard to hear and even more difficult to experience. What we must learn to come to grips with is that we and God view time quite differently. Yet that is a good thing. The worst thing that could happen for us is if God gave us all of our awards while we are on earth. For the few people that live to age one hundred, that is still so finite in comparison to eternity. Trust me that we want God's view of time operative in our lives.

Let me provide some more practical examples. We appreciate slow growth in many other situations in life. For example, it is so frustrating how quickly weeds pop up in our lawns. One day the grass is green and healthy, and the next day, it is full of weeds. Don't you wish the infestation happened a lot more slowly? Perhaps you already figured out where I am going. Healthy growth takes time, while unhealthy growth happens instantaneously. This is not an absolute, but I share this to encourage you if you have been in a holding pattern. Holding patterns are when planes are unable to land and therefore have to circle the landing area until further notice.  It is a position of waiting and waiting and waiting. That is what it feels like in moments where God is taking His time. However, the right perspective puts things in perspective.

*Holding patterns are necessary to get
us safely to our destination.*

Earlier this year, I took my daughter in for an eye exam. They had all of the new machines that optometrists use to examine vision. There were four different machines they used for her eye examination. My daughter had to answer several questions about what she could or could not see. One of the machines she would look through, and they would adjust the focus to strengthen her vision. The doctor would ask my daughter as she looked through the machine, "Does that make it better or worse?" My daughter would tell her when she could see more clearly. Another point worth mentioning was that the doctor and I could see what my daughter was looking at very clearly because it was projected on the wall behind her. We knew when she was seeing clearly based upon her reading correctly what was on the wall. She was at a disadvantage because, although we all were looking at the same thing, our view was much clearer than hers.

Did you catch that? God often makes us wait. **He makes us wait to help us see what He already sees from His perspective.** He moves slow but not because He loves us any less. Instead, He is trying to help us get on the right page, so we can experience what He knows is truly best for us. Here is the second reason God moves slowly. *He moves slowly because He wants to help bring our lives into focus on what truly matters.*

God's vision is much clearer than ours. The challenge and beauty are that God graciously causes time to work to our advantage even in moments of waiting. Even when things are moving slowly, it is still for our good.

I want to make sure you grasp this. I'd like to illustrate the third reason God moves slowly with another family story taught by my youngest daughter. About one year ago, my family and I had the privilege of taking an eleven-hour road trip to Florida. In all fairness, my daughters did a great job being in a car for eleven hours over a thirty-six-hour time period. However, a teachable moment came for me within the first ten minutes of our journey. After we left the house but before we even made it to the highway, my youngest daughter asked if she could have a treat. She was craving an icing-covered brownie. The only problem with her request was that it was 10:15 a.m.! My daughter, being an experienced negotiator, began to bargain on the appropriate time that she could be awarded the brownie. As we waited at a traffic light, she noticed a police car about twenty-five feet ahead. She then proposed her deal of a lifetime. Her request: "Daddy, can I have the brownie when we get past the police car?" My response: "No, it is still morning." Her rebuttal: "It is taking forever." Oh, the purification that happens through a family road trip.

My daughter had just taught me a theological truth that I had to spend much time contemplating: **our view of time is greatly impacted by age.**

*Our view of time is greatly impacted by age.*

To a six-year-old (at the time) child, thirty seconds waiting at a traffic light is a long time when waiting for what you crave. As a father, I thought that she had no clue how quickly thirty seconds would pass, or even thirty minutes. However, in that moment all she could see was that her temporary desire was not being met. I knew that I would eventually grant her request, but I would need to delay my answer to her request for a more appropriate time. (Ten minutes later…don't judge me!)

God is eternal (Ps. 90:2). He has no age and cannot be measured by time. If I, being wicked, know how to give good gifts to my children, then imagine what God has prepared for His children (Matt. 7:11). However, God is not shortsighted but looks through the lenses of eternity. He knows what we are experiencing and how those experiences will prepare us for eternity. I once heard a preacher say that eighty years of suffering pales in comparison to one second in glory (borrowed from Rom. 8:18).

For those ten minutes (again, don't judge me), my daughter pouted. When God is slow to respond or chooses not to answer my request, I sometimes respond like a six-year-old child and pout. I fail to see that God is working out something greater for my good, others' gain, and His glory that I may never see until I make it to heaven.

My question for you to ponder is this: Where are you? Are you experiencing God's swiftness or slowness? Whichever season you are in, know that God's grace is sufficient, and His love is unending. He loves you equally whether you are experiencing suffering or celebration. However, our response in both seasons is important. If you are in a season of celebration, you should be praising God for His goodness and looking for an opportunity to bless others. If you are in a season of suffering, you can still praise God for His goodness and look for an opportunity to bless others and be blessed by others. All of us would much rather be on the giving end rather than the receiving end. Yet there is joy on both sides when we approach these seasons with humility.

# GOD MATH AND TIME CHALLENGE

1. Try thanking God for what is good in your life rather than complaining over what is bad.

2. Write down how you have grown during difficult times.

3. Ask God for wisdom on what He wants you to see in your season of difficulty.

4. Ask God for wisdom to see what His will is in your season of celebration.

# GOD MATH AND RELATIONSHIPS

There is nothing that you and I are better at manufacturing for ourselves than God is able to produce. Notice I said "manufacture" and "produce." There is a major difference between those two processes. Let me further explain.

Manufacturing is something humanity excels at. From can goods to automobiles, we have become experts in the manufacturing process. Unfortunately, this mass production mind-set has seeped into our view and expectations of relationships. On an assembly line, mass production is fantastic. It is efficient, cost effective, and able to accomplish more, faster. However, none of these characteristics transfers over well when we seek to cultivate quality relationships. Manufacturing is about efficiency. In manufacturing, quality is often secondary to quantity. Yet God uses relationships to produce in us so much of the quality in our lives. When it comes to relationships, we must not elevate quantity over quality.

Expert farmers understand the value of waiting when it comes to fresh produce. It is not an overnight process. It requires patience and endurance. No true farmer plants a seed and expects a harvest the next day. Farming is laborious and costly. They also understand that part of the process is beyond their control and other parts within their control. It is important to learn how to leverage what you can control and let go of what you can't. This principle is perhaps ever so true in quality relationships.

There is a story in the Bible about a woman named Ruth. When Ruth steps on the scene, she is marked by tragedy. Her husband has died, which is a major ordeal during the era in which she lived. This would mean that her future was filled with uncertainty. On top of that, she was a Moabite who made a drastic decision to go live among the Israelites. Let's just say that her parents were displeased at best about her series of choices. However, from her story we are provided a magnificent portrait of God's ability to restore. Segments of the book of Ruth have been quoted at countless weddings in the exchanging of vows. Perhaps you have heard this famous line: "For where you go, I will go, and where you lodge, I will lodge. Your people shall be my people, and your God, my

God. Where you die, I will die, and there I will be buried. Thus may the Lord do to me, and worse, if anything but death parts you and me" (Ruth 1:16–17).

Talk about commitment. Now, before you check out, I want to highlight some of the drama that takes place in Ruth's story.

Ruth decides to travel with Naomi (her mother-in-law) despite her giving Ruth every reason to turn back. Yet Ruth is unwavering in her commitment to Naomi. It is a lot easier to read the ends of stories and draw the conclusions as if the main character knew he or she would have a favorable outcome. However, that mind-set robs the story of the author's intent. Ruth had no idea, other than faith, that things would work out as they did. Yet she travailed in hope that things could turn around for her. She was fully invested and held nothing back. Remember that prayer that I quoted earlier from Ruth's words to Naomi? She had the audacity to fully commit to someone who had little obligation to her.

We live in a day where commitment is so lopsided. It has become more about what you will gain from a relationship rather than what you will give. Relationships have become shallow and self-serving. Endurance has become a sign of weaknesses in relationships rather than of strength. We have been taught to enter relationships with the expectation that there is always an out. Happiness is one of the gods of this age. Yet what we fail to take into account is how unreliable and fickle we all can be. Please do not take offense, but let me plead my case.

I have discovered that I am so erratic that I do not even pursue my own good at times. I have been known to let myself down, so I know I will let other people down. There have been more times than I care to admit where I knew what was in my interest, and yet I chose what was easy. The cost of following through was greater than I was willing to pay in the moment. Maybe it was because of fatigue, laziness, or just plain rebellion, but my momentary desires got the best of me. I, like many, have had my share of letdowns but have also been the cause of letdowns. My humanity sometimes gets the best and makes the worst of me. Now, understand that this is not an excuse to become complacent. Rather, it is a reminder that we all have blind spots. So what are we to do about our struggle with unfaithfulness?

First, we must acknowledge that there is a problem. Alcoholics Anonymous has helped lead millions of people to freedom from bondage by that simple yet complicated first step. If people are unwilling to acknowledge that they have a problem, then they will never take the precautionary steps to resolve it. Are you aware of your blind spots? Blind spots are those kinks in our armor that display our weakness to everyone but us. If we are not aware of them, then we desperately need someone close enough to help point them out to us.

Awareness in these areas is pivotal to our growth and development. *We will never become who we were meant to be until we learn to face who we actually are.* This may be our greatest threat to our potential. There are few people who hurt you like you hurt yourself.

Second, we must become benefactors of grace. We let people show us who they are and choose to love them according to who they could be. **Deep relationships require dependent love.** There is a point where my love runs out, and I feel that I have little to give. Yet God in His gracious love for us has given us the Holy Spirit to live inside of us. Not only does He live inside of us but He also lives through us. This suggests that when we are asked to go beyond our capacity, there is still capacity available. When we are depleted, He is not. Paul had to learn this valuable lesson in 2 Corinthians 12. As he prayed for relief from his overwhelming circumstance, he learned a valuable truth about his God. "My [God's] grace is sufficient" (2 Cor. 12:9). This was a capacity beyond and greater than Paul's capacity. This was a strength, an endurance, and a source of power that went far beyond what Paul knew until this moment of desperate need. **There are some things that we can only learn about God in the negative.**

I remember eighth-grade math like it was yesterday. Though it was many decades ago, I remember it because it was the first time that I struggled with math. Before eighth grade, I loved a challenge and would welcome it in math like a starving kid meeting his favorite meal for lunch. Bring it on! However, in eighth grade, that changed for a moment. I was introduced to negative numbers, and for a while, this concept did not make sense to me. All my years prior, I had been taught that after zero, you stopped counting. This initially made math very difficult for me, because I had to come to accept that math could happen on the negative side of zero. There was a whole new world of math I would be exposed to upon embracing this math fact. So it is for the follower of Christ. There is an entire new realm of opportunities when we accept that God may be calling us into the negative, humanly speaking. *Yet it is during our exhaustibility that we discover His inexhaustibility.*

I would like to share a moment of transparency. I grew up in a single-parent home and was raised by a mother of amazing strength, wisdom, and godliness. She raised four children almost single-handedly. I did not meet my biological father until I was almost twenty-five years old. I never heard my mother tear down my biological father or shut the door to his involvement, but for whatever reason, he chose not to be involved in my childhood. Years later, as an adult, I had the chance to ask my father his reasoning for not being involved in my childhood. He chose not to provide one. He has never apologized or chosen to acknowledge any wrongdoing on his part. To be even more transparent, we still to this day do not have much of a relationship, even though I constantly reach out to him. He is often unresponsive and seems to care very little at all about developing a relationship, though I have told him that the door is wide open. I call him constantly and have gone months and even years without a call back after numerous attempts. I share this to say that Christ has given me a love for this person that my humanity wants me to throw away. I long to see him love and experience the love of the God who chose to keep me when I should have been thrown away. I do not have the capacity for that. To be honest, I find myself in the negative too often to admit, but God math works best in the negative.

There are some things that you cannot fully appreciate until you are under the weight of a load that is beyond your capacity to carry. I enjoy working out. I really enjoy running, but from time to time, I enjoy lifting weights. I am far from the strongest man in the world and probably not even the strongest on my block. However, in my home I am *the man*! My daughters believe that their dad is one of the strongest men in the world. Thank God for children to help boost the ego. We presently have a weight set in our garage. I remember years back when my daughters entered the garage as I was working out. They marveled at Dad's strength as I lifted one hundred plus pounds (don't judge me) up with ease. Their words to me at that time were, "Daddy, you are strong!" Children love to mimic their parents, so after I placed the weight back on the rack, they of course asked if I would allow them to try. I knew they were not able to handle the weight, so I made a deal. I pointed out a five- or ten-pound dumbbell nearby and gave them permission, with my spotting, to have a go at it. They eventually lifted the weight and felt proud of themselves. However, they could tell by examining with their physical eyes that the weight they lifted was much smaller than what Daddy had been lifting, which sat nearby on the rack. Their words to me were, "Daddy, you are *really* strong!" Their observation when they first entered the garage gave them an *image* of their daddy's strength. The weight looked heavy, and based upon their limited capacity, they could not imagine lifting the weight. However, when they struggled to lift weight much less than what they witnessed Daddy lifting, they now had an *experience* of Daddy's strength.

God's goal is to help us move from having an image of
His strength to having an experience of His strength.

God, in His love for us, will sometimes allow us to rest under the weight of heavy and draining relationships. **His goal is to help us move from having an image of His strength to having an experience of His strength.** There is something beautiful about God that can only be learned when we find ourselves under the weight of problems beyond our capacity to bear. It is then that we move from an image of God's strength to an experience of God's strength. There is a major difference between the two perspectives.

Now, back to the book of Ruth. I am sure it would have been easier for Ruth to be half in given her circumstance. However, her unwavering commitment to her mother-in-law is a model of God's ability to remember. Ruth would live in Bethlehem with her mother-in-law, Naomi, with much uncertainty. Yet God was at work behind the scenes. God was moving on the heart of a kinsman-redeemer named Boaz. A kinsman-redeemer was a relative who could step in to provide support to a family that was in crisis. There was a financial-assistance process God had instructed the families of Israel to set in place for families like Naomi and Ruth that might experience hard times. Boaz did some research on Ruth and learned about her faithfulness in serving her mother-in-law, Naomi. Upon hearing about her faithfulness to Naomi, Boaz took greater interest in Ruth. *Ruth stayed faithful with what she knew until God provided the insight on what she didn't.*

Relationships are so complicated because unlike concrete things such as money and possessions, our relationships drastically affect our emotional health. Money or material possessions can't heal a broken heart. If you live long enough, you will inevitably experience letdown or disappointment by someone you love. These moments are often unpredictable and leave us feeling vulnerable and perhaps even wounded. Yet these are moments that God can use to cultivate a Christ-like heart unlike any other experience. There is so much redemption found in pain when it comes to loving seemingly unlovable people. Perhaps the greatest lesson we learn is that *we are them.* Don't stumble over the literary complication of that statement. It seems as though every time I find it difficult to love or forgive someone, God has an interesting way of turning the spotlight on the deficiencies in my own life. I certainly feel as if I am growing in holiness each day. My life looks completely different from what it was five years or even one year ago. Yet there are still areas in my heart that I have a tendency to think are okay, but then God shows me that I am not okay. He pulls back the layer by sending difficult people for me to love into my life. Guess what? He does the same thing in your life. The opportunity we are presented with in moments like these is to trust the work and power of the Holy Spirit to guide us into levels of intimacy we thought not possible.

Colossians 3:11 raises the bar through the roof in relational quality in Christ. Paul lists the most unlikely people groups perhaps ever to live being brought together through Christ. Paul says, "A renewal in which there is no distinction between Greek and Jew, circumcised and uncircumcised, barbarian, Scythian, slave and freeman, but Christ is all, and in all."

What a bar he sets. These groups are polar opposites. Let me just provide some background on two of those groups mentioned, barbarian and Scythian. Not many people living today would take kindly being called a barbarian. You would likely feel offended if someone described you as barbaric. However, a Scythian was an entirely different level. If history is correct, then Scythians made barbarians look like innocent little children. I will not get too graphic, but some historians suggest that Scythians were so vile that they would make the scalps of their victims into cups. I will leave it at that. Paul now bridges the divide between these people groups to impress upon them and us the power of the gospel. *The gospel is powerful enough to turn haters into helpers and foes into family.* Imagine the impact this has on a watching world. These experiences are not something basic math can explain but that only God math can.

Don't hold back even when you are uncertain how things will work out. Now, allow me to provide a few boundaries about this statement. This is not encouraging you to step into sin or outside of God's will. Operate within God's boundaries. My first little tidbit I would like to encourage you to glean is this: plant seeds in hope that your relationships will flourish.

Be wise in your planting of these seeds. I am not encouraging you to enable people by giving in to both their and your detriment. There are times that love is demonstrated in a hard "no." Other times it is demonstrated through a hesitant "yes." A hesitant "yes" is when you have every reason to say no, but you sense the Holy Spirit telling you to say yes.

Second, brace yourself, because people are going to hurt you. Jesus said in Matthew 5:39, "But I say to you, do not resist an evil person; but whoever slaps you on your right cheek, turn the other to him also."

Talk about an unreasonable expectation. I'm not certain I am ready for that level just yet, but I know that it is a reality. Let me clarify that this does not encourage or support domestic abuse. Find support and local resources if you are in that type of situation. However, I do want to challenge us that Jesus is calling us to take a road less traveled—a road that sometimes leads to public embarrassment, broken hearts, and dare I say suffering. Yet, through this we discover the God math that can only be experienced from the negative.

# GOD MATH AND RELATIONSHIP CHALLENGE

1.  What relationships have you giving up on because they seem so hopeless?

2.  Ask God to help you see what He desires for you to get out of these painful experiences.

3.  Who do you need to forgive? Who do you need to ask forgiveness from?

4.  Who are the people God has placed in your life that have been encouraging and supportive? Thank God for those people?

5.  How can you intentionally nurture those relationships?

# GOD MATH AND MONEY

God needs my money. That is what too many people believe. Now, they probably would find it difficult to actually say that. However, when they are asked to part with their money, then their hearts tell it all. They become defensive, guarded, and quite skeptical. Why is that? It is because we feel it belongs to us. After all, many of us work jobs we don't like to earn money to take care of our families or at least ourselves. In that we will have to give account for it, it does belong to us. However, it is not ours in the way we think. We are simply to be managers of it.

Now, my aim is not to get more money from you. However, I certainly want more for you, and the "more" I speak of, money can't buy. The "more" I speak of are the eternal riches scripture encourages us to store up for ourselves. I want you to be rewarded when it really matters. Now let's explore together how this works.

What too many people fail to understand about God is how generous He is. He is so generous that He actually encourages us to look out for our future. Unfortunately, His long-term view has a much longer runway than ours. When God suggests long-term planning, He truly means long (eternal) term. He encourages us to think and plan ahead even in financial matters. When God rebukes us for mismanagement of money or material possessions, it is because He does not want us to be so shortsighted. *We lack the ability to see as far into our future as God does.* We are very content with reaping all of our benefits while on earth. Yet God in His gracious wisdom tries to protect us from ourselves.

In Matthew 6:19–21, Jesus shares some wisdom on money management: "Do not store up for yourselves treasures on earth, where moth and rust destroy, and where thieves break in and steal. But store up for yourselves treasures in heaven, where neither moth nor rust destroys, and where thieves do not break in or steal; for where your treasure is, there your heart will be also." What we too often overlook is that Jesus does not rebuke us for storing up treasures. He only challenges us to store them in a secure place.

Think about it this way. At one point in time, Enron stock was worth lots of money. As a matter of fact, many people unfortunately suffered because of unethical and covetous practices. Those who held stock were able to leverage their investment portfolios to gain massive wealth and material possessions. However, once the scandal came to light, stocks plummeted, and wealth was lost. What had once provided financial security and stability was now useless. The problem was never in the people's desire for wealth; the kink in the armor was that wealth was the chief end. When wealth is the chief end, it takes on a Godlike influence in our lives. Money is amoral but the greed in our hearts wants to be satisfied. Unfortunately, the desire is so strong that it will be satisfied at any cost. That was the problem with the leaders of Enron. Thousands of people's lives were impacted by this scandal. When times were good, they were really good. However, when the truth came to light, there was unfortunately much regret. So it will be with those who fail to manage money God's way. They will discover how weak the god of money is. Money makes a terrible god.

That is why Jesus warns us. He does not forbid us from having wealth, but He does caution those who desire to get rich. We see this caution several times in scripture: "Make sure that your character is free from the love of money, being content with what you have" (Heb. 13:5) and "But those who want to get rich fall into temptation and a snare and many foolish and harmful desires which plunge men into ruin and destruction" (1 Tim. 6:9).

As I reflect on these verses, they lead me to a place of tension. I believe tension is a good thing, and when it comes to money, it is something we should consistently find present in our lives. It is tension in the area of money management that can lead us to bearing greater fruit for the kingdom and benefit for ourselves in the long run.

What is a better response to managing money? We must bring our hearts and minds to handle it with a longer view in mind. The Enron stocks lost their value as soon as it was discovered that the records had been falsified. Very few people would have thought that the company would have crumbled so fast. That is the reality of all earthly success. It is fleeting at best. These eighty or ninety years on earth are but a vapor (James 4:14). We are encouraged to enjoy them but not lose sight of the long game. Money management is one of the best ways to tell if someone is living with the long game in mind. There are certainly other ways, but money is probably the greatest way. Jesus said, "Where your treasure is, there your heart will be also" (Matt. 6:21). In other words, if we follow the trail where we place our treasure, we will find our hearts locked in that same treasure box.

Let me propose a new or old thought. God wants you to excel. He wants you to prosper. However, His idea of prosperity is often different from ours. Prosperity in God's economy is quite paradoxical compared to the world's. The world encourages us to make more and move up. Bigger is always a sign of better. Newer is the status symbol of success. However, in God's economy, success is not measured by how much we keep but rather by how much we give away.

Some of the most missed opportunities that followers of Christ fail to take advantage of are the ones created by how we manage money. Think about it! If there was a noticeable difference between how you manage money and how your non-Christian family, friends, coworkers, or neighbors manage theirs, imagine the automatic witnessing opportunities that could be created. For example, you get a promotion, and they ask what you are going to do with your increase. Instead of saying the same old, "I am buying a new car or a new house or taking a vacation," imagine telling them that you are increasing your giving to a local mission for orphans or you are taking a mission trip to serve those in poverty or you are increasing your support for a ministry effort at your local church. That turns the conversation from "Wow" to "Why?" That creates an automatic witnessing opportunity. People can argue with the words through our mouths, but they are powerless against our witness through our lifestyle.

*When was the last time your spending habits led to a witnessing opportunity?* If it has been a while, start thinking about how to adjust moving forward. I love how Randy Alcorn, in his book *Treasure Principle*, says, "God prospers us not to raise our standard of living, but to raise our standard of giving." What if we started managing money with that view in mind? Imagine the impact we could make on a world watching. Could this be what is missing from our faith? Might this be one of the most untapped evangelism strategies? When I read about the birth of the church in Acts 2 and 4, there was a compelling witness that these first-century followers of Christ had. We know it was the work of the Holy Spirit, but it was undeniable how that same Holy Spirit transformed their view of material possessions. This led to an undeniable witness from the watching world.

I come from a family of quite meager means. To be honest things were a struggle as I grew up and still can be from time to time. There are times when I wrestle with God over why the resources are not coming in as I feel they should. Perhaps you have had the midnight conversations with God, asking Him to make the supernatural happen by morning in your bank account. Like me, perhaps you have prayed for your money to stretch like the manna God provided for Israel during their time in the wilderness. Financial challenges have been spiritually forming for my family and I. I have learned to pray more diligently during times of economic instability.

This has impacted my prayer life in ways that I could not put a price tag on. However, I stumbled upon something profound about my shortsightedness a couple of years back. I discovered that I pray vigilantly during times of lack, not only asking God for the financial means to meet my perceived need but also for wisdom on how to better steward what He has provided. Then God shows up in various ways, and until recently, I would miss the greater spiritual lesson. Then I stumbled upon the greater lesson to be gleaned. The intervention and guidance I seek during times of famine is the same intervention and guidance I should seek during times of feast.

*The intervention and guidance
I seek during times of famine
is the same intervention
and guidance I should seek
during times of feast.*

It is easy to blame God during times of lack and yet fail to consult God during times of lavishness. God wants to guide us during both seasons. I don't have a problem asking for help when I am desperate, but what about times when I think I have things under control? That is the real test of trust. As a parent, I would feel insulted if my daughters only consulted me about their financial matters when they were in a bind—if during times of abundance, they could care less about insight from Daddy. I would feel as if something went wrong in my parenting. Now, God is the perfect parent and never questions His own judgment because it is always just. God's justice supersedes our fairness. I, on the other hand, am limited in my perspective because I want fairness. Well, I want fairness when it benefits me. Let's be honest: we do not really want fairness. If life was truly fair, how many speeding tickets would we have? How many diseases would we have? How many children would we have? How many jobs would we have lost? Hopefully, you get my point. We don't really want fairness until we know it will benefit us. What we really seek is favor.

God is always working behind the scene to transform our hearts, which is some of the greatest work He does. Money is a fantastic way that He does that. The worst thing God could do is immediately bail us out of our financial dilemmas. This would not be good for us or for others. Now, before you shut this book (or burn it), let me explain. At least hear me out because you paid for it (hopefully).

There is a story recorded in 2 Kings 4 where this widow approaches Elisha. Now, Elisha was a big deal during his day. He was a prophet of the Lord and the successor of the world-famous Elijah. This widow was in a difficult situation. What is interesting to note is that this widow's husband was seemingly a faithful servant of the Lord. As a matter of fact, he feared the Lord. However, he left his family in significant debt. Debt back then is something we know very little about in our Western culture. Debt then, as in many other countries around the world, had to be repaid. You could not file bankruptcy and start over. Someone had to pay. They would make your children slaves until the debt was paid off. On top of that, women had few rights in that culture, so their hopes of survival were locked in their children (hopefully male children) to bail them out. Therefore this was double jeopardy because her children were about to be taken. Now, 2 Kings 4 tells us that she presses her way to Elisha and tells him of her dilemma. Elisha asks a penetrating question that tells a lot about what God is up to. He asks, "What do you have in the house?"

The woman replies, "Nothing in the house except a jar of oil."

Did you catch that? She said "nothing," but then she said she had something. You can't have nothing and something at the same time. Only one can be true.

I identify with this widow too often. I too quickly gravitate toward what is going wrong rather than what is going right. I am too quick to focus on what is deficient rather than what is sufficient. I hone in on what is missing rather than what is available. Like this widow, my heart is hardwired to concentrate on what I wish I had rather than maximizing what is readily available. From God's intervention in this widow's life, we discover a powerful truth about ourselves. There is nothing that we are better at providing for ourselves than God can. This woman's husband knew Elisha; now this woman would get to know this God of Elisha up close and personal herself. It was never just about a payment, but it was always about a person.

As the story unfolds, this woman is told to go and borrow vessels, as many as she could find, and then go shut the door and start pouring the oil. She does what Elisha commands, and she watches a miracle unfold before her very eyes. Please don't miss this: the person who was after this widow's heart was God. Elisha was only a willing instrument, bearing witness to the power and all sufficiency of this almighty God. This woman is freed from her bondage and brought into freedom by the intervention of a loving God. So much truth is wrapped up in that reality, but I will hold off until the end to unpack.

It is never just about money; it is always about who is our master. Money so wants to be our master and for many serves as just that. However, money makes a terrible ruler. Yet this lifeless idol is so persuasive and enslaves men and women to lives that never truly lead to joy. Unfortunately, few actually discover this reality until it is too late. Hopefully, it can be different with you and me. I challenge you to put money in its place. Money makes a terrific servant but a terrible god. We have to consistently contend to keep money in its place. Like a rebellious two-year-old throwing a tantrum in the grocery store aisle, it will not go quietly but often goes kicking and screaming to its destination. Yet we must have the spiritual resolve to not give in and assign money to places of eternal impact. If we are not vigilant, then we will look up and find ourselves paying more than we could afford to pay and staying in a situation longer than we wanted to stay.

On the other hand, money makes a terrific servant. Think of all the good that has and can be done with money. Wells can be dug, bridges can be built, vaccines can be given, gardens can be planted, and the list goes on and on. Thank God for governments, but that was never God's plan for the poor to be provided for. Christians have always been charged with defining their lives by acts of mercy and serving vulnerable populations. In too many cultures, this has now become the government's job and has become the Christian's excuse for overlooking needs. Spiritually speaking, we have been laid off from our Christian responsibility. This is a subtle way in which we allow money to become our master. We excuse away our responsibility for meeting the needs of others. After all, there are government programs or nonprofits for that. Do I actually believe that excuse will work with God? Look, my goal is not to condemn us, but it is to convict us. There is so much more we can do when we dethrone money as our god. There is also so much more God can do in our hearts when we dethrone money as god.

Think of the people, organizations, companies, and families that are waiting on you to be unleashed to make money do what it was purposed to do in your hands. There is something powerful that happens when money is in the hands of one being guided by God.

That is why it is important that you and I give. We give not to get but to be transformed. It is through our giving that we truly learn what it looks like to follow Jesus. Each time I give money away, I am declaring with my heart that covetous living is not who I am. Rather, Christ is my life. I am declaring (sometimes timidly) that God owns and controls it all. I am putting my confidence in God and not the all-weakened dollar. I am sending my treasures ahead to be deposited in my eternal account that will never perish. I am actually unlocking joy that comes from someone and something greater than this world can offer. I am saying that God alone satisfies.

Please do not miss the truth of that conclusion. God alone satisfies. I will be honest and admit that this is often easier to declare than it is to live. I have to constantly remind myself that when facing uncertainty. I have to declare that to myself time and time again. Yet it is the foundation of a life in Christ. In Colossians 3:4, Paul declares, "When Christ, who is our life, is revealed, then you also will be revealed with Him in glory." That is a powerful anchoring truth for us who follow Christ. The following verse, which seems dark when read alone and out of context, bursts into life-giving meaning after we read verse 4. Paul says in verse 5, "Therefore consider the members of your earthly body as dead to immorality, impurity, passion, evil desire, and greed, which amounts to idolatry." Paul, in a short summary, is saying, why reach for death when you already have life? He is not just saying a mediocre life but rather a glorious life. Think about it; Christ always did things greater. In John 2, He did not just turn water into a similar wine but into a better wine (John 2:10). In John 6, He does not just feed the crowd but satisfies the crowd "as much as they wanted" and still has leftovers (John 6:11–13). The point I am attempting to make is that you and I cannot satisfy ourselves anywhere close to the satisfaction God brings through Christ. Try sending your treasures ahead, and according to Jesus, you will not be disappointed.

# GOD MATH AND MONEY CHALLENGE

1.  Commit to setting a part of your earnings to give away to kingdom endeavors.

2.  Start seeking God's guidance during times of feast and famine.

3.  Start writing down testimonies of how God provided or how you were able to bless others.

4.  Seek financial counseling from a godly man or woman who has experience in managing money well.

# GOD MATH AT ITS GREATEST

Of all the math God does, the greatest is the gospel. Too often we limit God's impact on life to temporary work He does. While those are things we should certainly celebrate, they only provide small glimpses into the grander work God has done on our behalf. We should always marvel at the tangible ways that God miraculously intervenes in our lives. The times where our resources seemingly multiply by the end of the week—praise God for them. The situations where you exceeded not only their expectations of you but your expectation of yourself—praise God! The diagnosis that left both you and the doctors astounded—praise God! The unexpected refund or promotion or grade or proposal—praise God for each of those. The child who turned his or her life around when you had given up...the spouse who kicked that destructive habit...I could go on for days about the obvious ways that God has shown up in my life and the lives of others. I could fill this book with testimonies of my life alone. In the words of John 20:30, "Therefore many other signs Jesus also performed in the presence of the disciples, which are not written in this book."

Miracles of tangible resources—physical, relational, or mental health—and all the wonderful blessings God graciously allows us to enjoy are all setups. They provide minor glimpses to prime our hearts for the greatest work God has done: the work of salvation. Of all the God math, our salvation is *the greatest*. All else pales in comparison.

Christ's sinless life, sacrificial death, and irrefutable resurrection are the climactic benefit of God math. Imagine, if you will, saving for a long-awaited trip to visit the Grand Canyon. You have been waiting for years to experience this wonder of the world. You have saved and sacrificed, and finally you are prepared to make the journey across the country to experience this epic natural wonder. After twenty hours of travel, you can see the signs counting down the miles before you stand on the edge of the Grand Canyon. You are now in the final minutes of approaching the canyon. You have just passed the final sign that shares the Grand Canyon is one mile away. You brace yourself and prepare to be awed at this massive wonder. To make final preparations, you pull into a nearby souvenir shop. They have some really great deals, so you rack up on postcards, portraits, T-shirts, coffee mugs, and even wall-mounted pictures of the Grand Canyon. You are having the time of your life in the souvenir shop. You have had such a great time that you feel that there is no longer a need to press a couple of meters ahead to experience the Grand Canyon itself. Therefore, you pack up all of your memorabilia and head back home.

Now, I know you are thinking that would be absurd. Who would ever be so foolish? Yet how many people experience the miracles of Jesus, and they stop short at the miracle of food or healing and miss the greatest miracle Jesus offers—salvation? *Don't settle for the portrait and miss the most grandiose experience.*

In John 11 we find this amazing story of Jesus raising Lazarus from the dead. Now, this was no ordinary resurrection. Lazarus was completely dead. They have already had the funeral, and by now four days have passed. There is not even an ounce of hope to see Lazarus again by now. There is only regret of what could have been had Jesus gotten there in time. Martha and Mary are deeply saddened by Jesus' detachment from them at perhaps their most vulnerable hour of need. Jesus has healed many others by now. He at least could have spoken a word from where He was as He did in Matthew 8:8 with the centurion's servant. However, Jesus does nothing. He waits and waits and waits and waits! Lazarus dies, and Jesus still is not there. Finally, Jesus shows up after Lazarus

has been dead for four days. Can you imagine what Martha
and Mary were thinking? What they were feeling? I'd imagine
they felt very similar to how I have felt in seasons where Jesus
seemingly let me down. Martha poses perhaps one of the
most honest statements in scripture: "Lord, if You had been
here, my brother would not have died" (John 11:21).

Yet Jesus is loving and gracious in how He responds to
Martha during this time of unimaginable sorrow. To fast-for-
ward into the story, Jesus would ultimately summon Lazarus
back to life by calling Lazarus by name. Can you imagine
standing in the crowd in that moment? You are watching them
roll the stone away and seeing a man who you know was dead
because you saw his lifeless body with your own eyes. He was
not just dead but dead and buried for four days. Jesus stands
outside his tomb and calls his name, and he comes walking
out of the tomb. What would that do for your faith? Would you
believe that Jesus is all that He has declared Himself to be?

Perhaps you have not come to the place where you have
accepted Jesus Christ as your Lord and Savior. Maybe you
feel that if you had a little more evidence, then you would
believe. If you had one more miracle, you would cross the
line of faith. Allow me to push the envelope, if you will. In
the story I shared earlier, which is recorded in John 11, we
discover something extremely interesting about the response
of the crowd that witnessed the resurrection of Lazarus. John
11:45–46 says, "Therefore many of the Jews who came to

Mary, and saw what He had done, believed in Him. But some of them went to the Pharisees and told them the things which Jesus had done."

Praise God for the many that came to believe. Yet if you read it too fast, you will miss an unbelievable reality noted in the passage. There were some in the crowd who still did not believe. As a matter of fact, they went back to share with the Pharisees what Jesus had done, stacking a case against Him. In John 12, it goes on to say that not only did they start plotting to kill Jesus but now they wanted to kill Lazarus as well. How unbelievable is that? There is a potent point that John presses throughout his Gospel. My friend, miracles alone will not convince you of the saving power of God's gracious work of salvation. **We come to God by faith alone, in Christ alone.** What is the reality gap that is preventing you from believing in the sufficiency of Jesus Christ's death, burial, and resurrection as the atoning work for forgiveness of your sin? Perhaps you feel that one more miracle would help you to believe. I would suggest that maybe it will, or maybe it could be the very reason you refuse not to believe.

Coming to Jesus does not mean that all doubt goes away. I have met some of the most godly people who still wrestle with doubt on some level. **Faith is not the absence of doubt but rather trusting in Jesus despite of it.** There are moments when we will doubt, though we love and trust Jesus and God works with and through that. This is different from sheer unbelief in Christ's finished work on the cross as sufficient for my forgiveness.

John 11 highlights a beautiful stretching of Martha and Mary's faith. Martha, upon hearing that Jesus had made it to town, runs out to meet Him. She pours her heart out about her disappointment in Jesus's timing. They then enter into a theological discussion about the resurrection. However, Martha misses the irony in her dialogue with Jesus. Martha is theologically talking about the resurrection to the Resurrection. Imagine how funny this conversation would seem in hindsight. *Hindsight has a funny way of turning our moments of extreme disappointment into moments of extravagant devotion.* The gospel is God's stake in the ground that His math works!

Another beautiful truth that Martha learns is that her plan for Jesus is always smaller than Jesus' plan for Jesus. She knew that Jesus could heal the sick, but she was not as confident that Jesus could raise the dead. Isn't it funny how in our humanness we have a tendency to believe that our plans for Jesus are better than Jesus' plans for Jesus? The human heart is too easily satisfied with a limited view of God's power. We limit God's power to material possessions, physical health, or flourishing relationships, which are important yet still limited. Those are so short of the greatest math God does. The greatest is revealing to us a Person, and that is the Person of Jesus Christ. I am not speaking of a fragile and weak Jesus, but I am speaking of Hebrews 1:3 bio of Jesus: "And He is the radiance of His glory and the exact representation of His nature, and upholds all things by the word of His power."

I am talking about Colossians 1:16–17: "For by Him all things were created, both in the heavens and on earth, visible and invisible, whether thrones or dominions or rulers or authorizes—all things have been created through Him and for Him. He is before all things, and in Him all things hold together."

I point you to Jesus' words in Revelation 22:13: "I am the Alpha and the Omega, the first and the last, the beginning and the end."

*My friend, you have plans for Jesus, but rest assured they are smaller than Jesus' plan for Jesus.*

Remember the story I shared earlier about Ruth? She rides off into the sunset with her hero, Boaz. Yet Ruth's greatest legacy is not that she was a faithful servant and was found by her dream man. Her greatest legacy is that she became part of the bloodline of Jesus. The greatest legacy that you and I will leave is not that we built massive cathedrals, rescued orphans, erected shelters for those in poverty, discovered cures for terminal diseases, raised productive citizens, educated students, changed the world… you fill in the blank on what success looks like. All of these are noble accomplishments and certainly things we should strive for. Yet our greatest legacy will not be the work that we do but our security in what Christ has done. Luke 10 records a remarkable teachable moment for the disciples by Jesus. Jesus launches them out into ministry with clear instructions on what to do. The disciples launch out and experience epic success. Jesus calls them into a ministry-debriefing meeting, and they began to rejoice over their ministry success. Their excitement is uncontainable. Then in verse 20, Jesus gives this staggering warning: "Nevertheless do not rejoice in this, that the spirits are subject to you, but rejoice that your names are recorded in heaven."

**Our greatest legacy is that we are treasured by Jesus Christ.** Wherever you are right now as you read, allow that truth to wash over you. You may feel like a complete failure. Everyone may have given up on you. You perhaps question your value. My friend, Jesus loves you deeply and is waiting on you to trust Him completely. He has this marvelous way of turning disappointment into divine setups. Will you trust God to do the greatest God math in your life, not increasing your possessions, nor increasing your time, and not even enhancing the quality of your relationships? The greatest God math is God taking a billion true accusations against us, which rightly leave us guilty and condemned, yet transferring them to His Son on the cross. Through Jesus Christ, all of our sins have been settled by one. I know of no other mathematical equation where:

$$1 > \infty$$

But with Jesus Christ!  Let that sink in for a moment. Perhaps you are not familiar with the "∞"symbol. It is the mathematical symbol that represents infinity.  Infinity at its simplest form means without end or to help us wrap our head around it, grows arbitrarily large.  As illogical as the mathematical hypothesis may sound, it becomes a fact when Jesus enters the equation.  The major truth I hope you will grasp is that Jesus is greater than any charge against you.  Any mistake, any fumble, any failure, Jesus sets it right. When Jesus enters the equation, we always end up with the advantage.  Sometimes that advantage may feel like a disadvantage, but rest in the truth that God causes all things to work together for the good of those who love God and are called according to his purpose for them (Rom. 8:28). However, too often we stop short and fail to understand what that good is.  That good is that we might be conformed to the image of His Son (Rom. 8:29).  No matter the number, the size, the scale, the accusation on the other side of us, God uses it to bring about a greater plan so much greater than we could have ever imagined.  The beauty of God math is that it displays the love and profound wisdom of God. God not only cancels our sin debt, but also gives us what we do not deserve. May this leave us astounded and constantly running toward a loving person, Jesus Christ, Son of God!  Get to know that person and watch God do math that transforms both you and the world around you.

# Gospel Challenge

1. Have you trusted Jesus Christ for your salvation? Have you placed your faith in Christ finish work on the cross as the atonement for your sin? Read these Scriptures: Rom. 3:23; Rom. 6:23; Rom. 10:9

2. Confess to the Lord where you are struggling to believe. Read Mark 9:14-29

3. Pause to reflect on God's amazing grace through the Gospel. Ask God to restore unto you the joy of your salvation. Read Psalm 51

4. Connect with a local church near you. You perhaps have more questions than I have provided answers. There are some Christians God has placed in your context that would love to help you grow.

# CONCLUSION

I never thought this day would come. I had no desire to read for many of my early years, so writing was completely out of the question. The book you hold in your hand or on your electronic device is a result of God math. The beautiful joy of having a relationship with Jesus Christ is that He gives you the desires of your heart. Unfortunately, too often we limit that truth to Jesus answering our every prayer with the outcome we desire. If you have ever prayed then you have come to know that is not true. A more accurate understanding is that Jesus will put the appropriate desires in our heart. These are desires that are for our good, others gain and God's glory. For example, I have witnessed this play out by God giving me a desire to pastor a church. The only career path I remember saying I would never do, during my adolescent years was, pastoring a church. Today, there is nothing else I'd rather be doing. Why? It is because God knows how to give us the desires of our heart. He put that there. God is so wise that He knows the number of hairs upon our head (Luke 12:7). He is so close that He knows what we should and should not ask for (Rom. 8:26).

This is what I want for you and more importantly what God wants for you. I want for every person reading this book to experience abundant life. I want your families and friends to also experience that abundant life. That abundant life will not be found in better things, better titles, better relationships, better fitness, or any other "better" that your heart is longing for. The abundant life you seek is found in a person, Jesus Christ. Coming to know Him leads us into that abundant life. Coming to know Jesus is the greatest mathematical phenomenon.

I started off by defining God Math as the undeniable intervention of God in ordinary situations. It is when ordinary people obey God in ordinary ways and experience extraordinary outcomes. That only happens as we get to know a person. That happens as we follow Jesus.

# 30 Days of Reflection

Set aside 5 minutes each day to write what you learned. The aim is not to fill each page but to create a habit of reflecting and journaling how the Lord is at work in your life. Don't give up if you miss a day, but pick up where you left off. Know that God desires to meet with you simply because He loves you.

# DAY 1

# DAY 2

# DAY 3

# DAY 4

# DAY 5

∞

# DAY 6

# DAY 7

# DAY 8

# DAY 9

# DAY 10

# DAY 11

# DAY 12

# DAY 13

# DAY 14

# DAY 15

# DAY 16

# DAY 17

# DAY 18

# ∞
# DAY 19

# DAY 20

# DAY 21

# DAY 22

∞

# DAY 23

# DAY 24

∞

# DAY 25

# DAY 26

# DAY 27

# DAY 28

# DAY 29

# DAY 30

# ABOUT MILTON

M ilton is a pastor, author, speaker, philanthropist and accomplished track and field athlete. In his track days as a professional athlete, he represented team USA at 6 IAAF World Championships – brining home 1 world record, 3 gold medals, and 3 silver medals. He has a B.A. from UNC at Chapel Hill and two Masters Degrees from Luther Rice University. He presently serves as Lead Pastor of The Midtown Bridge Church in Atlanta, GA. Milton has a passion for helping men and women discover and leverage their Kingdom potential. He is married to Christina and they have two amazing daughters. To learn more, visit www.inthexchange.com to see what he is up to.

54724684R00065

Made in the USA
Columbia, SC
08 April 2019